SUPER SIMPLE MAKERSPACE STEAM CHALLENGE

CREATE A ROCKET!

And More Flight Challenges

Megan Borgert-Spaniol

Consulting Editor, Diane Craig,
M.A./Reading Specialist

Super Sandcastle

An Imprint of Abdo Publishing
abdobooks.com

abdobooks.com

Published by Abdo Publishing, a division of ABDO, PO Box 398166, Minneapolis, Minnesota 55439. Copyright © 2021 by Abdo Consulting Group, Inc. International copyrights reserved in all countries. No part of this book may be reproduced in any form without written permission from the publisher. Super SandCastle™ is a trademark and logo of Abdo Publishing.

Printed in the United States of America, North Mankato, Minnesota
102020
012021

Design: Kelly Doudna, Mighty Media, Inc.
Production: Mighty Media, Inc.
Editor: Liz Salzmann
Cover Photographs: Mighty Media, Inc.; Shutterstock Images (boy)
Interior Photographs: JPL Caltech, p. 6; Matti Blume/Wikimedia Commons, p. 12; Mighty Media, Inc., pp. 10, 11, 15, 16, 17, 18, 19, 20, 21, 22, 26, 27, 28, 29; NASA/Johnson Space Center/Flickr, p. 7 (satellite); Official SpaceX Photos/Flickr, p. 7 (rocket launch); Senior Airman Codie Trimble/US Air Force, p. 7; Shutterstock Images, pp. 4, 8, 9, 10 (sponge), 13, 23, 24, 25, 28 (boy), 30; Space Exploration Technologies Corp./Wikimedia Commons, p. 13 (Starship)
Design Elements: Mighty Media, Inc.; Shutterstock Images

The following manufacturers/names appearing in this book are trademarks:
Craft Smart®, Duck Tape®, Glue Dots®, Scotch®, Sharpie®, Westcott®

Library of Congress Control Number: 2020940301

Publisher's Cataloging-in-Publication Data
Names: Borgert-Spaniol, Megan, author.
Title: Create a rocket! and more flight challenges / by Megan Borgert-Spaniol
Description: Minneapolis, Minnesota : Abdo Publishing, 2021 | Series: Super simple makerspace STEAM challenge
Identifiers: ISBN 9781532194375 (lib. bdg.) | ISBN 9781098213732 (ebook)
Subjects: LCSH: Handicraft for children--Juvenile literature. | Building--Juvenile literature. | Rockets (Aeronautics)—models--Juvenile literature. | Flight--Juvenile literature. | Engineering—Juvenile literature. | Mathematics—Juvenile literature.
Classification: DDC 745.5--dc23

Super SandCastle™ books are created by a team of professional educators, reading specialists, and content developers around five essential components—phonemic awareness, phonics, vocabulary, text comprehension, and fluency—to assist young readers as they develop reading skills and strategies and increase their general knowledge. All books are written, reviewed, and leveled for guided reading and early reading intervention programs for use in shared, guided, and independent reading and writing activities to support a balanced approach to literacy instruction.

TO ADULT HELPERS

The challenges in this book can be done using common crafting materials and household items. To keep kids safe, provide assistance with sharp or hot objects. Be sure to protect clothing and work surfaces from messy supplies. Be ready to offer guidance during brainstorming and assist when necessary.

CONTENTS

Become a Maker — 4
Challenge: Flight — 6
Challenge Extended — 8
Gather Your Materials — 10
Real Aerospace Engineers, Real Challenges — 12
Challenge Accepted! — 14
Challenge 1: Cosmic Tour Craft — 15
Challenge 2: Fifteen-Foot Flight — 17
Challenge 3: Cargo Carrier — 19
Challenge 4: Air Rocket — 21
How Did You Do? — 23
Get Inspired — 24
Helpful Hacks — 26
Problem-Solving — 28
A New Day, A New Challenge — 30
Glossary — 32

BECOME A MAKER

A makerspace is like a laboratory. It's a place where ideas are formed and problems are solved. Kids like you create amazing things in makerspaces. Many makerspaces are in schools and libraries. But they can also be in kitchens, bedrooms, and backyards. Anywhere can be a makerspace when you use imagination, inspiration, **collaboration**, and problem-solving!

IMAGINATION

This takes you to new places and lets you experience new things. Anything is possible with imagination!

INSPIRATION

This is the spark that gives you an idea. Inspiration can come from almost anywhere!

Makerspace Toolbox

COLLABORATION

Makers work together. They ask questions and get ideas from everyone around them. **Collaboration** solves problems that seem impossible.

PROBLEM-SOLVING

Things often don't go as planned when you're creating. But that's part of the fun! Find creative **solutions** to any problem that comes up. These will make your project even better.

CHALLENGE: FLIGHT

Have you ever been on an airplane or watched one soar through the sky? Have you ever seen videos of rockets **launching**? Airplanes and rockets are products of aerospace engineering.

Aerospace is made up of Earth's atmosphere and the space beyond it. Many people **design** and build **vehicles** that travel through aerospace. These people are called aerospace engineers. Aerospace engineers face challenges every day.

MEET AN AEROSPACE ENGINEER

Anita Sengupta is a rocket scientist and aerospace engineer. She worked at **NASA's** Jet Propulsion Laboratory in California. Sengupta helped land the Mars *Curiosity* rover in 2012. The rover flew toward Mars at 900 miles per hour (1,448 kmh). Sengupta helped design the parachute that slowed the rover's descent!

Aerospace engineers build rockets that **launch** into space.

Aerospace engineers make **satellites** that orbit Earth.

Aerospace engineers **design** airplanes, including military aircraft.

7

CHALLENGE EXTENDED

Aerospace engineers are challenged by demands. Demands are needs or desires that must be met. Aerospace engineers are also challenged by limits. These might be time limits or space limits. Aerospace engineers might also be limited by what materials they can use. The key is figuring out how to meet demands while working within any limits.

Are you ready to be an aerospace engineer in your makerspace? Read on to find out how the challenges in this book work!

HOW IT WORKS

THERE ARE FOUR CHALLENGES IN THIS BOOK. EACH CHALLENGE PRESENTS A TASK TO COMPLETE.

THE TASK WILL COME WITH AT LEAST ONE DEMAND OR LIMIT. THAT'S WHAT MAKES IT A CHALLENGE!

EACH CHALLENGE WILL HAVE MORE DIFFICULT DEMANDS AND LIMITS THAN THE LAST. THAT'S WHY IT'S A GOOD IDEA TO START WITH CHALLENGE 1 AND WORK UP TO CHALLENGE 4.

MORE MINDS

Invite others to tackle these challenges with you! You can work together as a group. Or, you can work individually and compare results.

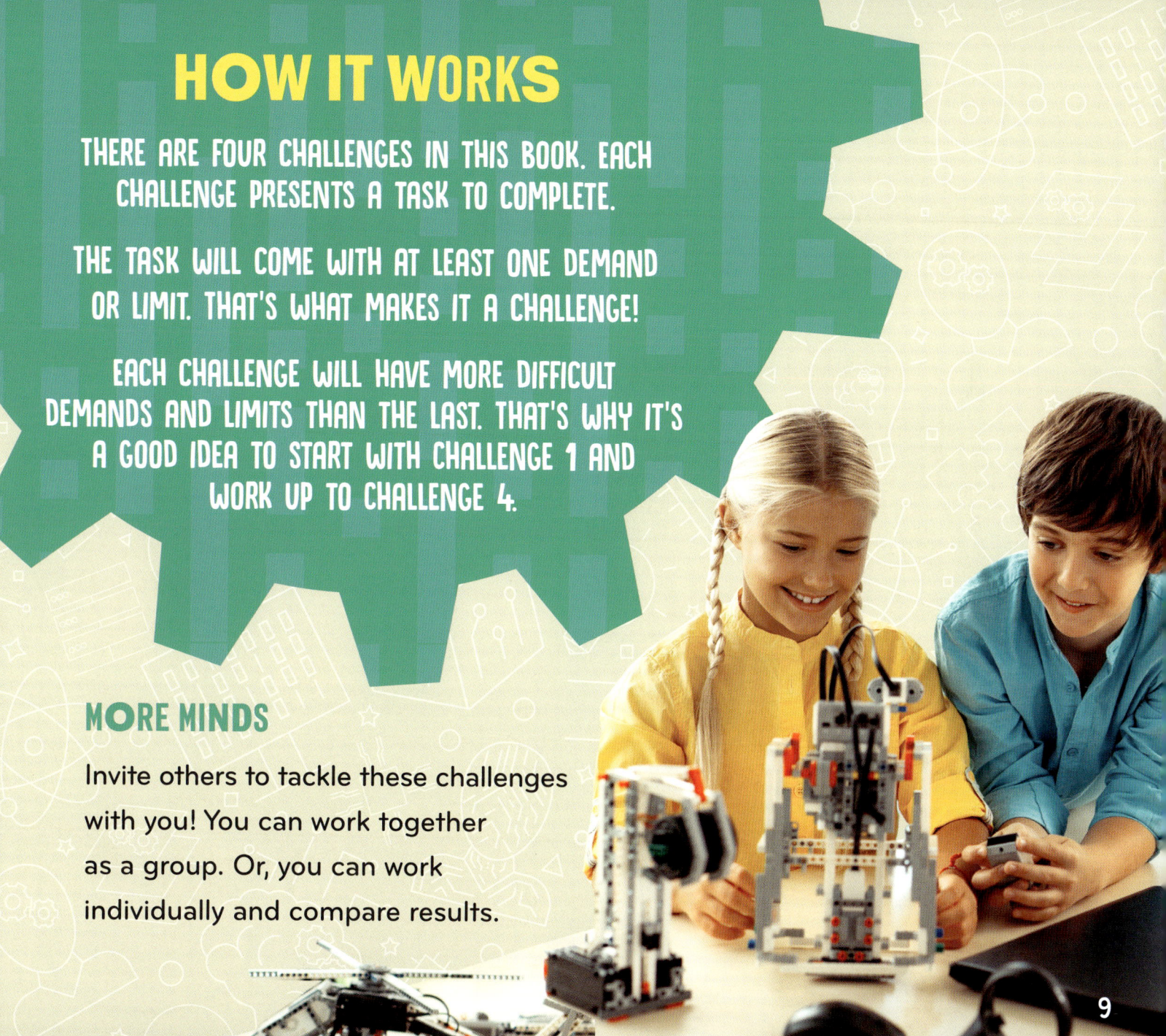

RULER

GLITTER

PLASTIC TUBING

GATHER YOUR MATERIALS

There are a few materials you'll need to do the aerospace engineering challenges in this book.

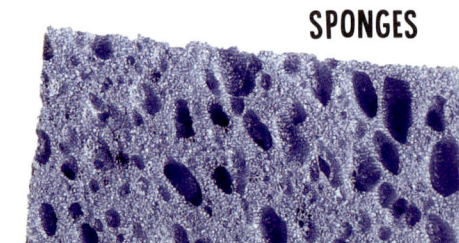
SPONGES

IMAGINE

IT'S UP TO YOU WHAT ADDITIONAL MATERIALS YOU USE. EVERY MAKERSPACE HAS DIFFERENT SUPPLIES. WHAT'S IN YOUR SPACE? GATHER MATERIALS THAT YOU CAN USE FOR STRUCTURE, CONNECTING, AND DECORATION.

STRUCTURE

These materials provide your creation with shape and support.

CONSTRUCTION PAPER

SCISSORS

FOAM PAINTBRUSH

WOODEN SKEWERS

CONNECTING
These materials help connect the different parts of your creation.

DECORATIONS & DETAILS
These materials add fun **details** that make your creation stand out.

REAL AEROSPACE ENGINEERS, REAL CHALLENGES

Before you take on your flight challenges, get inspired! Start by discovering some real-world challenges that aerospace engineers have faced. Check out the amazing results of these challenges!

CHALLENGE: MAKE AIR TRAVEL MORE AFFORDABLE AND ENVIRONMENTALLY FRIENDLY.

RESULT: ALICE, THE WORLD'S FIRST ALL-ELECTRIC COMMUTER AIRCRAFT. ISRAELI COMPANY EVIATION AIRCRAFT INTRODUCED ALICE IN 2019.

CHALLENGE:
CARRY PEOPLE AND **CARGO** TO THE MOON, MARS, AND BEYOND.

RESULT:
STARSHIP, A POWERFUL **LAUNCH VEHICLE** BUILT BY AEROSPACE COMPANY SPACEX. THE COMPANY BEGAN TEST FLIGHTS IN 2020.

CHALLENGE:
BRING HIGH-SPEED INTERNET TO EVERY CORNER OF THE WORLD.

RESULT:
ORBITING **SATELLITES** THAT TRANSMIT INTERNET DATA TO COMPUTERS ON THE GROUND. ONEWEB AND OTHER COMPANIES HAVE LAUNCHED THOUSANDS OF INTERNET SATELLITES INTO ORBIT!

IMAGINE

CAN YOU THINK OF OTHER POSSIBLE **SOLUTIONS** TO THESE CHALLENGES? WHAT IS THE WILDEST IDEA YOU CAN COME UP WITH?

HERE'S SOME ADVICE FOR TACKLING THE CHALLENGES IN THIS BOOK:

1. **LOOK BEYOND THE MAKERSPACE.** The perfect material might be in your garage, kitchen, or toy chest.

2. **ASK FOR HELP.** Share ideas with friends and family. Ask them for their ideas. Starting with many minds can lead you to places you'd never go on your own!

3. **THINK IT THROUGH.** Don't give up when things don't go exactly as planned. Instead, think about the problem you are having. What are some ways to solve it?

4. **BE CONFIDENT.** You may not know right away how you'll meet a challenge. But trust that you will come up with a **solution**. Start every challenge by saying, "Challenge Accepted!"

Do you have the materials you need? Are you inspired by the work of aerospace engineers? Then read on for your first challenge!

CHALLENGE 1:
COSMIC TOUR CRAFT

TASK: Design a model of a spacecraft for sightseeing across the universe.

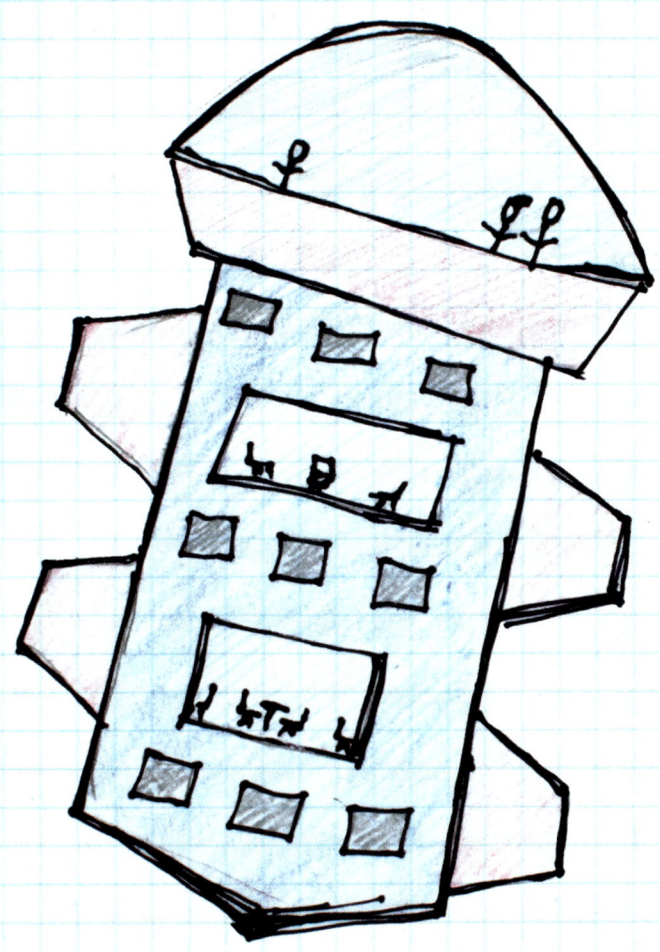

DEMAND
The spacecraft must include many windows for space travelers to look out.

LIMIT
The model can't be shorter than 12 inches (30 cm).

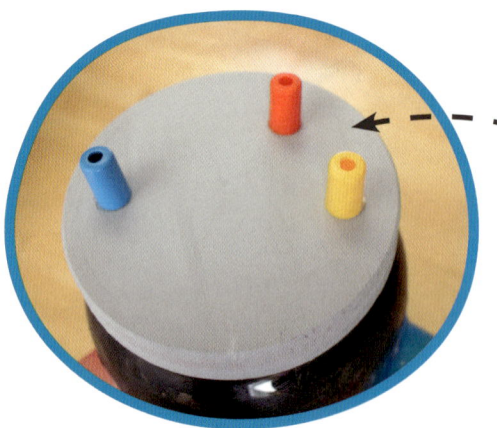

Observation deck and space **tourists** made with bubble wrap and plastic pegs

Zero-gravity pods let tourists float like astronauts!

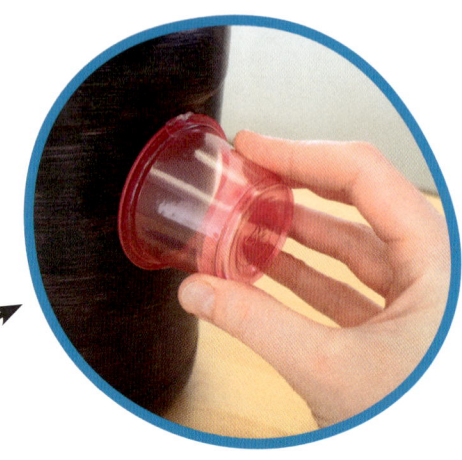

Reflective tape represents windows.

Black paint mixed with glitter to look like a reflection of outer space

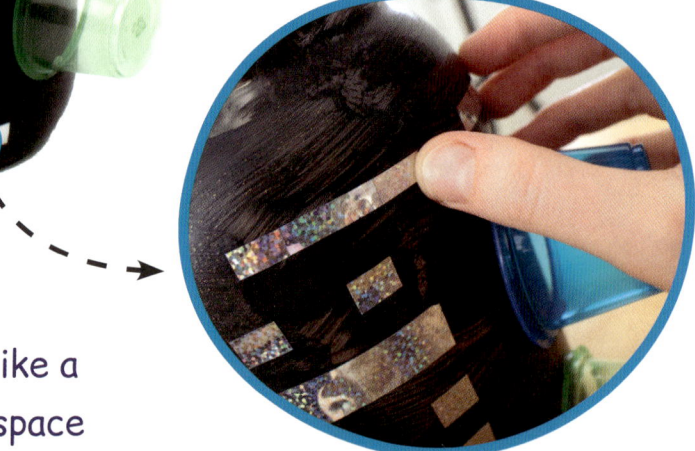

CHALLENGE 2:
FIFTEEN-FOOT FLIGHT

TASK: Construct an aircraft. This can be a helicopter, airplane, or glider.

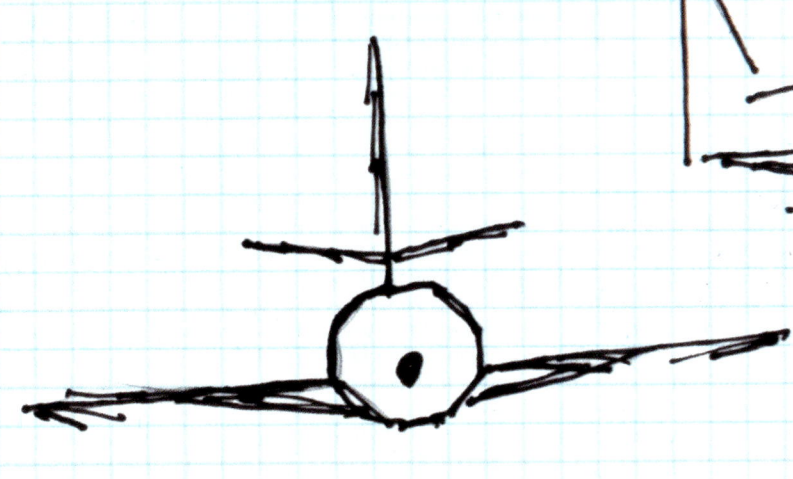

✓ DEMAND
The aircraft must remain airborne for at least 15 feet (4.5 m).

✗ LIMIT
You must build and successfully fly the aircraft within 60 minutes.

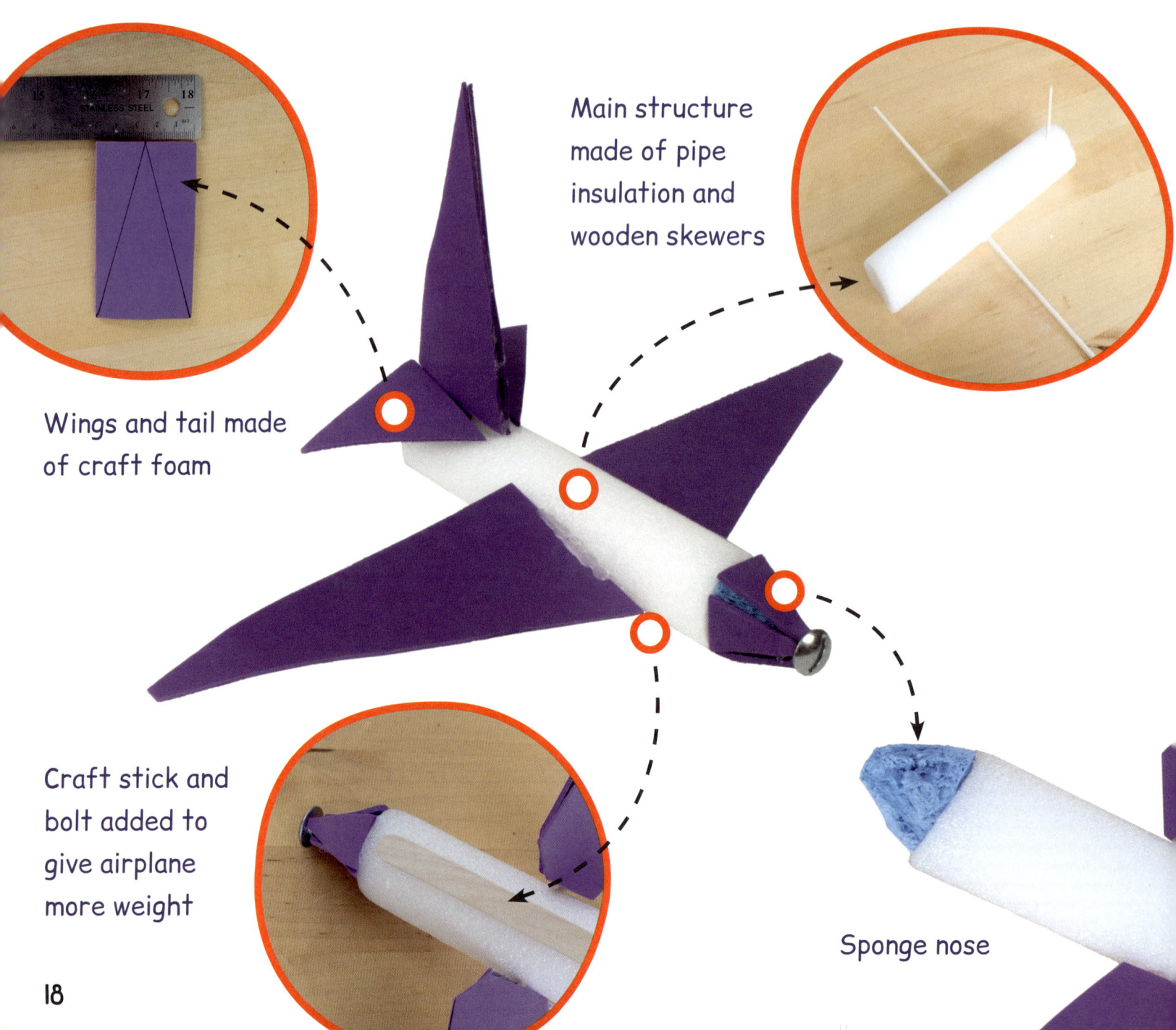

CHALLENGE 3:
CARGO CARRIER

TASK: Engineer a **cargo** plane.

✓ DEMAND
The airplane must support at least 2 ounces (57 g) of cargo weight.

✓ DEMAND
The airplane must soar in a straight line for at least 10 feet (3 m).

✗ LIMIT
The airplane can be made of no more than two different structural materials. This does not include connecting materials or decorations.

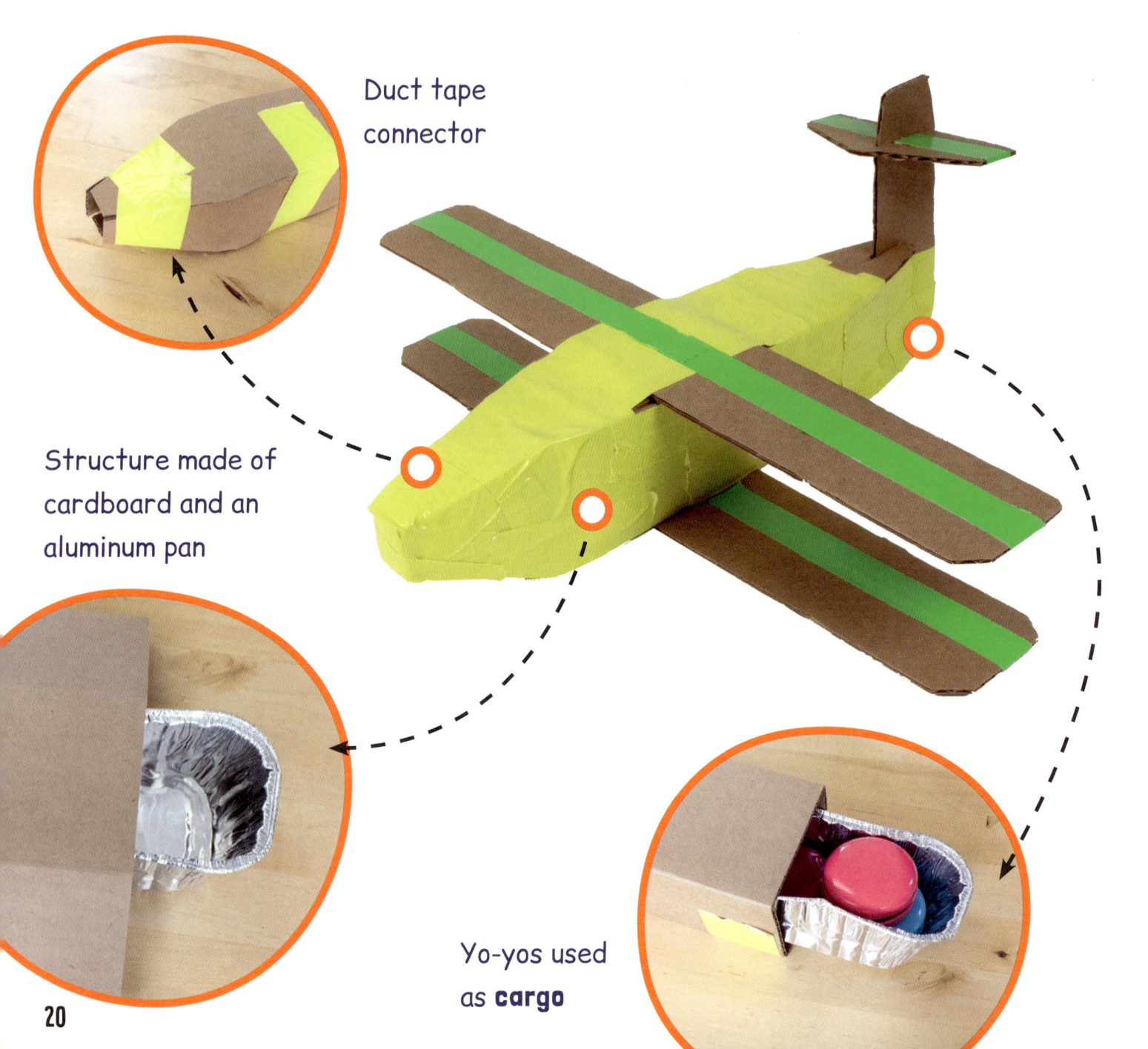

Duct tape connector

Structure made of cardboard and an aluminum pan

Yo-yos used as **cargo**

CHALLENGE 4:
AIR ROCKET

TASK: Build and **launch** a rocket.

DEMAND
The rocket must be **propelled** by a sudden force of air. This could be from a balloon, a bottle, or even your own lungs!

DEMAND
The rocket must launch at least 6 feet (1.8 m) into the air.

LIMIT
You must build and successfully launch the rocket in 75 minutes or less.

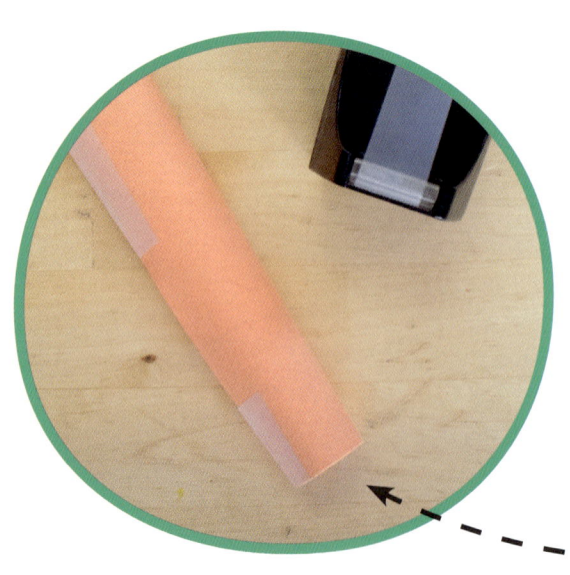

The air travels from the tubing into a lightweight rocket.

The air travels through plastic tubing. Duct tape provides an airtight seal around the plastic bottle and tubing.

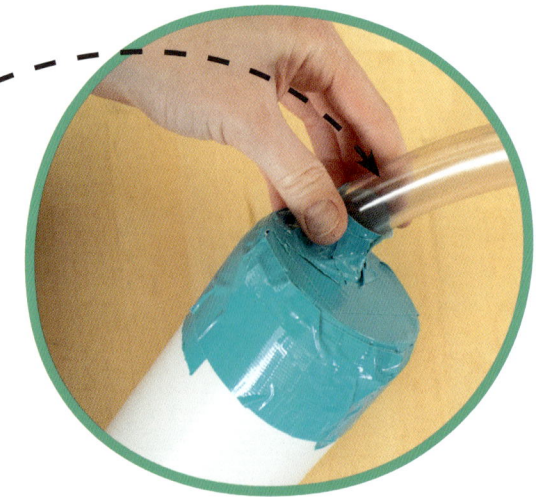

A **flexible** plastic bottle holds air. When you step on the bottle, the force pushes the air out.

HOW DID YOU DO?

After you've completed each challenge, think about how it went.

WHAT IS ANOTHER WAY YOU COULD HAVE APPROACHED THE SAME CHALLENGE?

WHAT WAS THE MOST DIFFICULT PART OF THE CHALLENGE?

WHAT WOULD HAVE MADE THE TASK EASIER?

WHAT KINDS OF PROBLEMS CAME UP, AND HOW DID YOU SOLVE THEM?

GET INSPIRED

As a makerspace aerospace engineer, you can find inspiration nearly anywhere. This will help you approach your challenges with a ton of ideas!

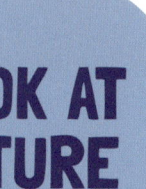

LOOK AT NATURE

An albatross can glide for thousands of miles without flapping its wings. Bats can fold their wings into different shapes. Bees adjust their wing beats to fly in windy conditions. Aerospace engineers often base their **designs** on these and other animal fliers!

24

LOOK AT EVERYDAY PHYSICS

Aerospace engineers use laws of **physics** every day. Look at examples of physics in your own daily life. You experience a drag force when you try to close an umbrella on a windy day. Gravity is at work when a thrown ball lands back on the ground. **Friction** helps you run on the ground without slipping.

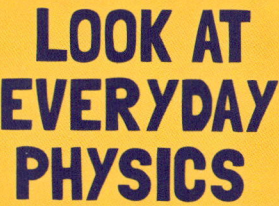

LOOK AT VEHICLES

Aerospace **vehicles** share many features with those on land or water. Race cars are **designed** to reduce drag. Motorcycles are highly **maneuverable**. Speedboats are lightweight. Which of these features could you borrow for your aircraft or spacecraft?

HELPFUL HACKS

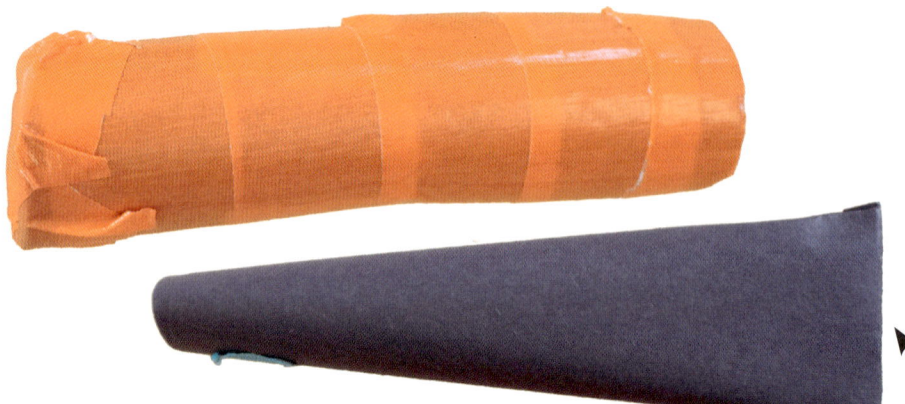

As you work, you might discover ways to make challenging tasks easier. Keep these simple tricks and **techniques** in mind as you work through your aerospace engineering challenges.

Test different rocket **designs** to learn which shapes and materials work best.

Carefully cut shiny tape with a craft knife on a cutting pad to make small windows.

Cut **slits** in cardboard to connect multiple pieces.

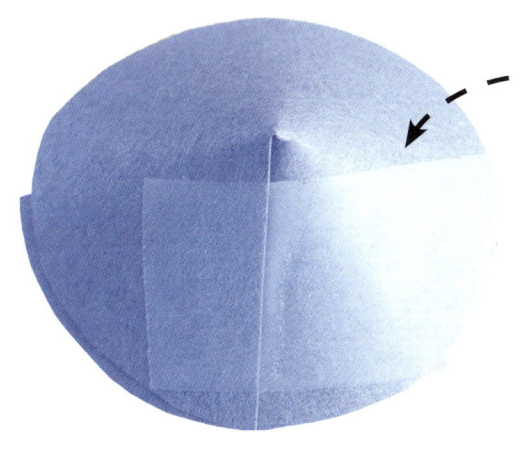

Create a rocket's nose cone by cutting a circle out of paper. Then cut a **slit** from the edge of the circle to the center. Overlap the two sides of the slit and tape them in place.

Trace one piece to make others that are the same shape and size.

Carefully use a sewing needle to poke a hole through foam. This makes it easier to push a wooden skewer through the foam.

PROBLEM-SOLVING

You'll probably run into problems as you attempt the challenges in this book. Instead of giving up, open your mind to new ideas. You'll likely find more than one **solution** to your problem!

PROBLEM
Your airplane isn't soaring far enough.

THINK
Why is this happening? Maybe the airplane doesn't have enough **lift**.

BRAINSTORM AND TEST

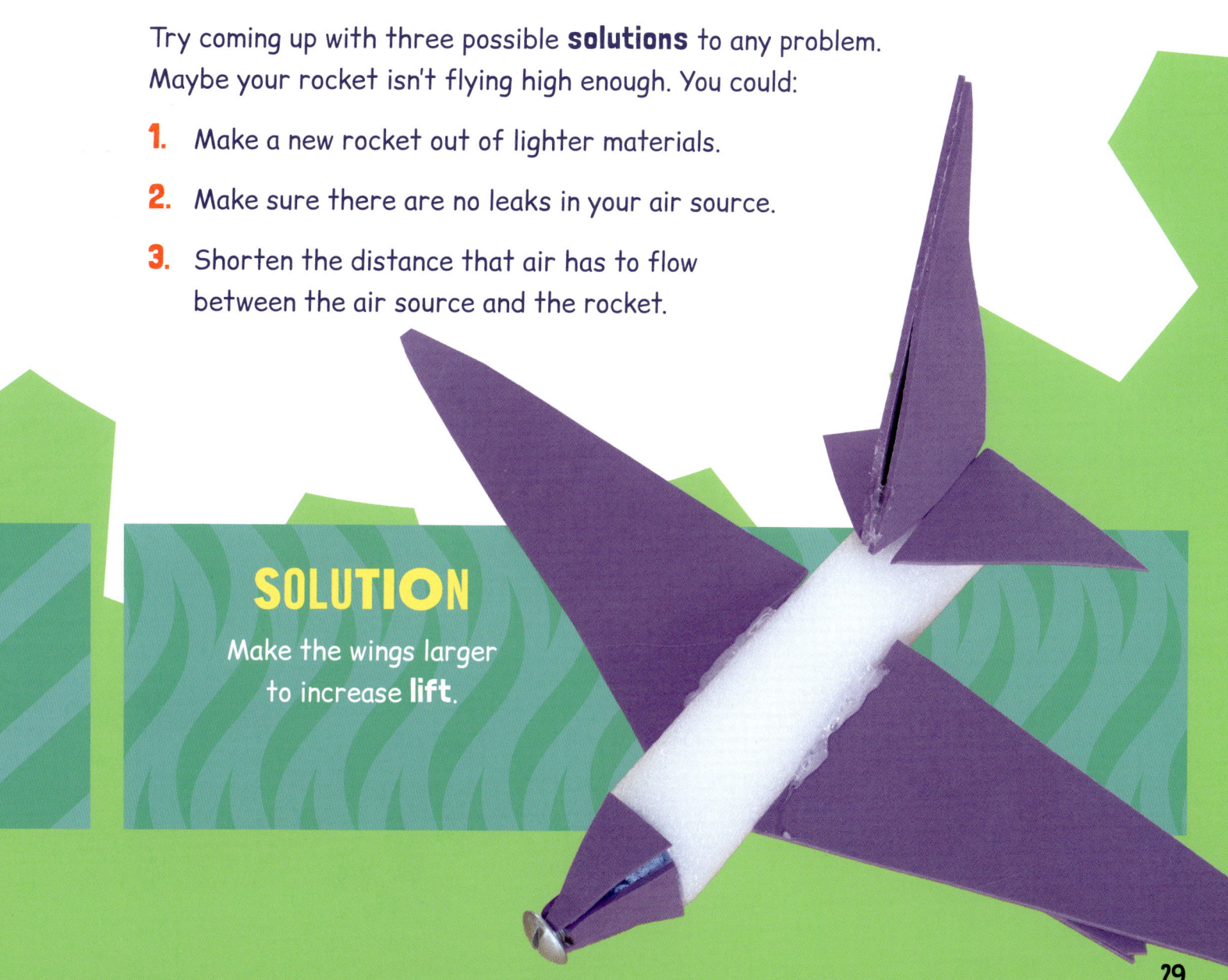

Try coming up with three possible **solutions** to any problem. Maybe your rocket isn't flying high enough. You could:

1. Make a new rocket out of lighter materials.
2. Make sure there are no leaks in your air source.
3. Shorten the distance that air has to flow between the air source and the rocket.

SOLUTION
Make the wings larger to increase **lift**.

A NEW DAY, A NEW CHALLENGE

If you had trouble meeting a challenge, try it again another day with fresh ideas. And if you did meet a challenge, still try it again! There is always more than one way to do something. Give yourself new demands and limits to give the task a new twist.

BEYOND THE MAKERSPACE

You can use your makerspace toolbox to take on everyday challenges, such as flying a kite or **launching** water balloons. But aerospace engineers use the same toolbox to do big things. One day, these tools could help build space colonies or make air travel cleaner. Turn your world into a makerspace challenge! What problems could you solve?

GLOSSARY

cargo – goods carried on a vehicle.

collaboration – the act of working with another person or group in order to do something or reach a goal.

design – to plan how something will appear or work. A design is a sketch or outline of something that will be made.

detail – a small part of something.

flexible – easy to move or bend.

friction – the resistance between two surfaces that are touching each other.

launch – to send something high into the air or into outer space.

lift – the upward force on an airplane's wings that opposes the force of gravity so the airplane can fly.

maneuverable – able to be moved in different ways or directions.

NASA – National Aeronautics and Space Administration. NASA is run by the US government to study Earth, our solar system, and outer space.

physics – the science of how energy and objects affect each other.

propel – to cause to move forward.

satellite – a manufactured object that orbits Earth.

slit – a narrow cut or opening.

solution – an answer to, or a way to solve, a problem.

technique – a method or style in which something is done.

vehicle – something used to carry people or objects. Cars, trucks, boats, and airplanes are vehicles.